DARTMO SETT MAKERS BANKERS

By
SIMON DELL and JOHN BRIGHT

THE DARTMOOR COMPANY

First published in 2008 by The Dartmoor Company,
The Coach House, Tramlines, Okehampton,
Devonshire EX20 1EH   Telephone 01837 54727

British Library Cataloguing in Publication Data.

A catalogue record for this book is available from the British Library

ISBN 978-0-9555150-1-9

Design, layout and typeset by:-
Simon P. Dell

Editorial by:-
Jocelyn Bright

Printed and bound in Great Britain by:-
The Printing Press, 21 Clare Place, Coxside, Plymouth, Devonshire, PL4 0JW

Cover photographs:-
Sett Makers' Bankers on the eastern slopes of Middle Staple Tor. (Simon Dell)

CONTENTS

ACKNOWLEDGEMENTS

Firstly our sincere thanks go to Helen Harris who has written prolifically on the subject of Dartmoor's Industrial Archaeology. She kindly shared a wealth of information with us from the outset of our researches and was unfailing in her encouragement.

Both the Duchy of Cornwall and Maristow Estates Office have been most generous in allowing aerial photographs of their lands to be included in this publication.

Kath Brewer has been of immense support with regard to the Foggintor area where she grew up as a child; and the late Ted Fitch of Dartington was a constant source of advice and sound judgement about suspected bankers.

Peter Stannier kindly made his drawings of the sett makers' tools available for copying. His published work on Dartmoor Granite was of immense assistance to us.

The National Trust kindly allowed photographs to be taken at Castle Drogo of their excellent exhibition of bankers' tools.

Finally the late Louis Rich of Princetown, last manager at Swell Tor Quarry, who was of great practical help with first hand information and personal experiences of the sett making industry along with his great nephew, the late Rod Cooper, last manager at Merrivale Quarry. Both men enthusiastically supported the writing of this small record, and to both men we respectfully dedicate it.

4

1. INTRODUCTION

Many ramblers who have walked the slopes of Great Staple and Middle Staple Tors not far from Merrivale Quarry on the western side of Dartmoor, will no doubt have come across the curious remains of what was once a thriving industry. Small granite benches are located on the hillside, mainly to the south and the east of these tors.

Bankers on the eastern slopes of Great Staple Tor

(Simon Dell)

Some walkers might wonder what these strangely constructed remains were, curious as to their purpose. That industry was

5

actually the manufacturing of granite street cobbles, or 'setts' as they are more properly known. The ruins of the low benches, or 'bankers' are strewn across the hillsides in large quantities both here and elsewhere on Dartmoor as well as beyond on Bodmin Moor. They are a lasting testament to the moormen of the second half of the nineteenth century, who toiled long hours for poor pay, sometimes in atrocious weather conditions, to meet the ever increasing demand for these setts for the improvement and construction of streets in both nearby Tavistock as well as the busy port of Plymouth.

Early 20th century photograph looking down West Street, Tavistock with views towards Cox Tor in the distance showing relatively new kerbs and footpaths.
(Courtesy of the Dartmoor Archive © Devon County Council)

Nineteenth century Plymouth was a thriving and growing port with immense Naval importance and thousands of setts were used both inside the Royal Dockyard as well as outside its walls in the Devonport area. The town of Tavistock was undergoing a great revival in building owing to the influence of successive Dukes of Bedford since the 1840's. By the 1870's the demand for granite setts was so great that a whole manufacturing industry was dedicated to their production. This book looks at all the aspects of that industry and the men who worked in it. The various locations of the numerous remains will be visited, hopefully sparking

Granite setts used in a back lane in Tavistock

(Simon Dell)

some interest to encourage the reader to go out and discover the legacy that has been left behind. We have, over several years of research and exploration found hundreds of bankers in various locations but one thing is for sure, many still remain undiscovered. This book is not intended as a definitive list or account of their whereabouts; in fact we would welcome being made aware of any that we have managed to overlook in the course of our perambulations. Some people might have believed that the bankers are only located on the side of Great Staple Tor above Merrivale Quarry, but numerous others do exist near other quarries and also places where granite was freely available to be used by the sett makers.

Granite Setts used in a back lane in Plymouth.

(Simon Dell)

Before visiting the various remains in our following chapters, it might be useful right at the start to set the scene as to why this industry came about and to put the bankers into their rightful historical and social context. The bankers date from about the 1870's, although some authorities suggest 1850 – 1860. It is important therefore to look at what was going on at that time nationally as well as locally. Dartmoor is by no means unique in its own sett manufacturing.

The construction of roads had been going through its own revolution during the late 18th and early 19th centuries. The old roads could no longer cope with the increase of wheeled traffic as well as the size and weight of these vehicles. Traction engines were increasingly appearing on our roads and the old soft cart tracks and former turnpike roads were no match for the destructive capabilities of a powerful steam driven vehicle. The Industrial Revolution of the late 18th and early 19th centuries had placed enormous pressure upon the road network system of the country.

Late 19th century photograph showing a much worn Duke Street from Bedford Square, Tavistock.
(Courtesy of the Dartmoor Archive © Devon County Council)

At this time the streets of Tavistock and other nearby towns basically consisted of compacted earth and stone, which soon turned to mud during rainy periods.

Eventually pot holes appeared and numerous complaints were made by rate-payers and business proprietors about the state of the roads. Landowners as well as the local parish authorities were under pressure to do something about the woeful state of their highways. Likewise the road network in and around the dockyards in Plymouth was being churned up because of its poor construction so something had to be done to keep pace with the increase in traffic and size of vehicles, both mechanical as well as horse-drawn. A new road building material had to be sought with stronger capabilities than previously found, and locally we were well placed near Dartmoor with an abundance of granite.

The grand municipal building boom of the 1800's, especially in Tavistock and Plymouth, also demanded an increase in the use of granite for building and floor construction. Footpaths with kerbstones were becoming fashionable and this also needed construction material. Thus the taking of granite from the open moors increased tremendously. Until then the granite on the open moorland commons had mainly been the domain of local farmers and moormen whose ancestors had often 'robbed' antiquities and used the most convenient source of granite but this new demand would soon outstrip the previously utilised granite.

Prior to the opening of the numerous quarries on Dartmoor (Merrivale Quarry itself opened in 1875 but Foggintor had commenced operation much earlier) 'moorstone' - granite lying on the open moors - was worked to supply the needs of building material. Individual and suitable pieces were identified, cut and worked generally 'in situ' and evidence of the granite workers is strewn all over the moorland area.

Many Tors were robbed of their stone and when this natural, easily accessible resource had been significantly worked the task of digging the quarries commenced. Controls on the taking of granite were soon put into place by landowners with marker posts and signs erected to prohibit the removal of granite in certain areas. The horse-drawn tramways of the mid 19th century opened up the moors to this new large-scale industry. The bankers on the sides of Great Staple Tor pre-date the opening of the nearby

Moor stone split in two directions into blocks ready for the sett maker.
(John Bright)

Merrivale Quarry and utilised the abundance of this 'moorstone' granite lying on the surface of the moor. A great granite causeway was built along the eastern side of Great Staple Tor to gain access for wheeled vehicles used in the removal of the moorstone from the sides of the tor.

11

Above: Jack Warne, on the left, see using a 'jumper' bar in order to drill small holes in the granite block along the desired line of the intended split. The 'jumper' was made of iron with a bulbous middle with two sharp ends. When dropped, it could drill a hole for 'feathers and tares' within 15 minutes. The "feather and tares' consisted of two small wedges either side of a central 'tare'. A line of 'feathers and tares' would be inserted into holes and when tapped they would split the granite in two. On the right is Gilbert Hext of Princetown.
(Courtesy of David Cooper kindly arranged by Tom Greeves)

Below: A sett maker's hammer.
(Kindly loaned by Wesley Key, Buildings Supervisor of the National Trust at Castle Drogo)

Indeed the original purpose of Merrivale Quarry (known then simply as 'Tor Quarry') was for the construction of granite setts. Perhaps the demand for granite setts had out-stripped the ability of the sett makers to find suitable moorstone lying on the surface of the nearby hillside.

A solitary banker at the head of the granite causeway with
Great Staple Tor high above to the left.

(Simon Dell)

As will be seen within this small book, numerous bankers found near quarry workings actually post-date the earlier quarries and utilised spoil from the workings. Clearly the spoil was worth re-visiting for the purpose of sett making and also kerbstone manufacturing. The industry bridged the gap between some of the older quarries where the sett makers sought scrap granite to re-use and the necessity to

13

open Merrivale Quarry to keep up with the demand for stone. As with many aspects of social history on Dartmoor, the overlaps are immense.

The following chapters are going to look at the locations

of bankers, their construction and similarities; how the setts were made and the tools used in the work. We will look at the method of transporting the setts from the open moors and the locations where these setts eventually ended up being used. The purpose of this introduction was simply to set the scene for our following chapters, to show that with the increased demands placed upon our road system and building construction methods something new had to

Setts in Church Lane, Tavistock (Simon Dell)

be introduced. That 'something' was the introduction of the granite sett with its own specific and peculiar manufacturing process. If you have not seen any of the bankers for yourself and you are interested in following our journey of discovery over the following chapters then can we recommend an easy stroll across the hillside of Great Staple and Middle Staple Tors? You are no doubt going to come across quite a few of them on the eastern slopes above the quarry at Merrivale in the region of grid reference SX 545757. Having a basic idea of what they look like will help you considerably.

2. WHAT IS A BANKER?

Sett making on Dartmoor arose as a result of the demand for hard-wearing road surfaces in major towns such as Plymouth. The sett makers' bankers which represent the physical remains of the industry that arose to meet this demand are still to be found in a number of areas of the Moor. But exactly what is a "banker"? Helen Harris, in her informative article in the 1981 edition of the "Transactions of the Devonshire Association" describes bankers as:

" ... *low primitive benches formed against the hillside by the placing of two upright pieces of granite about 1 foot 6 inches [45cms] apart, and another slab across the top, approximately a foot above ground level. Men knelt or crouched at the bankers cutting small setts from larger blocks.*"

A fine example of a banker from high up on Middle Staple Tor.

(John Bright)

15

This definition is sufficient for general interest, and was certainly the most accurate to be found when we started to become interested in these strange little benches that had begun to feature so heavily in our Sunday walks upon the moor. However, the more we looked the more bankers we found, often in locations which we never expected and – as a pattern began to emerge – the more hotly was each pile of granite chippings debated. Is this pile of granite fragments the remains of a banker? How could we decide? It seemed sensible to look carefully at the data from all of the bankers we had found to date and identify their common features. We would then be in a much better position to decide what activity was represented by an abandoned pile of granite chippings.

We have found bankers in eight distinct areas on or around Dartmoor, although there are undoubtedly a number we have yet to locate. Their locations and the reasons behind them are subject of future chapters. Where bankers occur it is usual to find a number of them associated together within an area, although they do occasionally occur as isolated individuals.

A "typical" banker is constructed very much as Helen Harris has described: *"... it is a single bench 17" [35cms] high at the front (from current ground level), with an internal width of 17" [35cms], a dip of 40 degrees from horizontal on the working surface and 50 degrees from horizontal on the front face of the work surface. It was usually built facing upslope although a large number are associated with the interiors of quarries where there is no natural gradient."*

Considering the wide diversity of their locations, and the apparently random nature of their construction, bankers show – with only one or two exceptions – a remarkable uniformity of construction, as though they were built to a prescribed formula. Of the more than 70 bankers for which we collected data, height above current ground level varied the most ranging from 20cm to 75cm.

Pairs of bankers on the eastern slopes of Middle Staple Tor.
(Simon Dell)

However, given the nature of their use, the erratic distribution of spoil around the bankers – including very frequently beneath the banker itself – and the growth of vegetation subsequently, it is important that we evaluate how much ground level may have risen since the end of the nineteenth century when sett making was at its height.

On average the bankers that we examined had beneath them a cover of vegetation and underlying soil of 2cm to 4cm with a further 5cm to 8cm of granite chippings beneath that. This suggests that the tops of the bankers were between 8cm and 11cm higher above ground level than they are today.

Measurement of the angle of dip on the tops and front faces was often difficult because of the uneven nature of the surfaces, but again the range was limited to ten degrees either side of the average result. It seems reasonable to suggest that the purpose of arranging the top surface at an angle was to make working on the stone easier, and to prevent the debris collecting on the work area. The dip on the front face was markedly more erratic and showed a range from 25 degrees to 90 degrees from horizontal. Within that range distribution is fairly uniform, with the most common value being 45 degrees.

A number of bankers occur as singles very closely associated together, and others as pairs, triples or even quadruple bankers built together and sharing upright or top stones.

To date we have also found 6 pairs of bankers which have been built "back to back", separated by distances of nearly 1 metre, so that if used by two workers at the same time their backs would almost certainly have been touching. We will discuss how workers positioned themselves at these bankers later in this chapter.

As well as displaying many common features in their construction, bankers also demonstrate similarities in the aspects associated with their use. The debris of its use will mark the presence of a banker; the top of the bench and the immediate surrounding area are liberally covered in granite remains ranging in size from small 'grains' of 2 - 3 mm which occur close to the bench, and larger, angular remains usually found further afield to a distance of 1 - 1.5 metres Many of the larger fragments show at least one corner of 90 degrees. Also present in the field of larger debris are small numbers of "failed" setts where an error or unexpected weakness in the stone many have resulted in it splitting wrongly, leaving a finished product which would not have passed quality control.

Over half of all the bankers we examined had what were clearly small walls of less than 30 cm in height to the front of the banker. Where these walls exist the debris is usually contained within the walls. Whether they were built as an attempt to contain the waste or were associated with shelters long since perished cannot be ascertained. The spoil heaps associated with a small number of bankers show evidence that quantities of fine debris have been removed, possibly indicating that a use could be found for the waste.

Right: A short wall at the front of a banker, with debris retained behind it. The long grass is growing from the bench area.
(Simon Dell)

19

Left: A small granite shaker containing a compact single banker on the southern slopes of Middle Staple Tor.
(Simon Dell)

The fine grained, well drained material on the top of bankers provides ideal growing conditions for English stonecrop (Sedum anglicum), and with only a few exceptions each banker has a fine covering of this mat-forming plant (see page 33).

Dartmoor is at times a very inhospitable place, and it seems obvious that those people who had to work on the Moor found ways of gaining shelter from the worst of Dartmoor's weather. A few bankers still reside within well built stone shelters. The best of these are to be found tight under the South face of Middle Staple Tor, although the very best example is to be found built into a spoil heap opposite the South entrance to Foggintor Quarry. Other bankers are thought to have been sheltered by *"..sloping screens or 'shakers' – generally of galvanized iron..."* (Helen Harris 'Industrial Archaeology of Dartmoor' p.31) The picture on page 21 of granite stone dressers from Northern Ireland gives a good impression of how these temporary shelters may have looked.

The picture also suggests that men working at bankers would have knelt at the bench. Certainly the shape and height of the bankers lends support to the claims of several writers that *"The worker knelt in front of the banker and chiselled the stone...."* (Sandy Gerard's 'Dartmoor').

Sett Dressers cutting Morne Granite in temporary wooden shakers at Newcastle, County Down, Ireland, in the late nineteenth century. (Courtesy of the Ulster Museum Welch Collection)

A closer examination of the great majority of bankers on Dartmoor shows that this may well not have been the case. Beneath many of the bankers there are quantities of large angular granite fragments in the area where it would be expected that a kneeling worker would have placed his knees. Even allowing for the fact that these were tough men, and that time was certainly of the essence, it seems implausible that they would have allowed sharp debris to accumulate in a place where they were to regularly put their knees. Further, the act of kneeling for any prolonged period of time would have been very painful even without the attentions of quantities of sharp stone. It makes more sense to support

21

the suggestion that men would have stooped at these bankers with their knees resting against the front face of the bench. Certainly we found this position more comfortable than kneeling, and the use of tools (which we will discuss in a later chapter) felt easier.

So now whenever we see a curious arrangement of short upright stones, fragments and stonecrop upon the Moor we have a better chance of deciding whether we are looking at the remains of a banker. We also have a better picture of how it may well have appeared in use, with a man stood at the bench, looking down onto its sloping surface at which he was carefully shaping pieces of stone, protected from the worst of the weather by a shelter of stone or sheet iron, with the debris of his work around his feet and scattered in front of him, and in the company of a number of others similarly employed.

A banker protected by a granite 'shaker' wall below the north slopes of Middle Staple Tor.

(Simon Dell)

3. WHERE ARE THE BANKERS TO BE FOUND?

Although Moorstone has been taken for many centuries for use in construction, it was not until the early 19th century that anything which could be described as a granite industry developed. The industry arose as a result of demand for granite for bridges, docks and public buildings. As transport improved, demand also grew for better, durable road surfaces, in response to which stone workers on Dartmoor built themselves little benches or bankers upon which to manufacture the cobbles and kerbstones to surface the city roads. Although demand for cobbles to pave the city streets was high, these sett makers' bankers were only in use for a short period around the end of the 19th Century. These small remnants of a short – lived industry still remain on the Moor. But where are they and what are the reasons behind their locations?

Sett makers' bankers can be found in a number of different locations on Dartmoor: Foggintor, Swell Tor, Dewerstone, Leather Tor, Lowery Tor and Grenofen, although by far the greatest concentration is to be found scattered over the sides of Great Staple and Middle Staple Tors. Similar bankers have also been found associated with quarries such as Cheesewring on Bodmin Moor. Wherever they occur, bankers were always associated with commercial granite extraction, and usually with quarrying. So why are bankers only found in the areas around the West and South-West of Dartmoor?

23

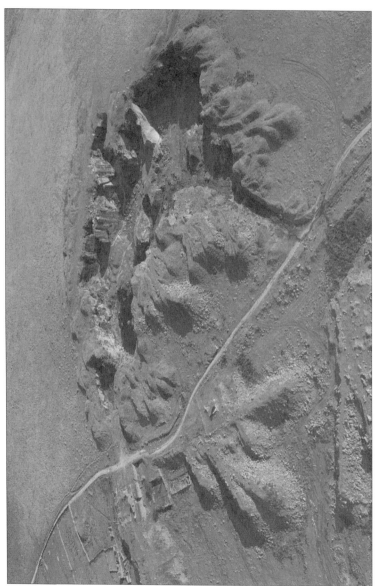

Most sett making on Dartmoor was associated with large-scale commercial granite extraction. A large number of bankers can be found amongst the spoil heaps of Foggintor Quarry.
(Simon Dell with kind permission of Maristow Estates Office)

The reasons for their uneven distribution can be divided into two main groups: geological and commercial.

The granite which outcrops at Dartmoor, Bodmin Moor and a number of other smaller sites in the South West was emplaced as a fairly fluid magma underneath much older Devonian and Carboniferous rocks during one of the final stages of the Variscan Orogeny (mountain building event) in phases between 300 and 270 million years ago. All of these granite outcrops are connected at depth to the Cornubian batholith. Recent technological advances have allowed geologists to map the extent of the batholith, even though only its tips outcrop at the surface. It varies between 10 - 26 km thick, and 40 - 60km wide at its base. In total it has been estimated that the batholith comprises over 68000 cubic km of granite.

Granites are intrusive igneous rocks (rocks formed from a molten liquid) composed of at least 10% visible quartz. As is the case with most igneous rocks granites are composed entirely of interlocking crystals, making them hard and resistant to weathering. Crystal size is strongly linked to the rate at which the melt cooled. The larger the crystals, the slower the rate of cooling. Under certain conditions of temperature and pressure white feldspar crystals grow within the melt, long before the other minerals begin crystallization, producing a Porphyritic texture. Outcrops of the Cornubian Granite at Lands End, Hensbarrow and Dartmoor have big feldspar granites, whilst Bodmin Moor, Carnmenellis and other areas of Dartmoor are noted for a more medium-sized texture with the majority of crystals being of approximately equal size. Most of the coarse and medium-grained granite areas have yielded good stone for building or engineering purposes.

One of the bankers within the Cheesewring Quarry near Minions on Bodmin Moor.

(*Simon Dell*)

The best stone is usually of a uniform medium grain because it can be evenly dressed and weathers well, being less susceptible to physical and chemical action. Granite quality improves with depth. Before opening a quarry to extract better granite, knowledge of the underlying geology was gained by examining outcrops and moorstones. In general the wider spaced joints lie beneath the tors. The granite might be unfit when discoloured around faults. Not all of the granite within a quarry is sound. There are several notable vertical pipes of rotten granite (growan) within Foggintor for example. Fine-grained granites, formed by a more rapid cooling at the upper margins and in subsequent veins, and those which bear a large percentage of feldspar phenocrysts resulting from particular temperature / pressure conditions within the molten magma chamber, do not split accurately with ease. However, there are a number of locations on Dartmoor where suitable medium to coarse grained granite appears at the surface or can be won from quarrying. To understand the uneven distribution of bankers we also need to analyse the commercial activities existent at the time.

Bankers occur in some quite unexpected places. Barely visible beneath the moss is a banker by the elvan quarry west of Grenofen Bridge. (Elvan is a fine type of crystalline granite).

(Simon Dell)

27

There has long been a tradition of using granite for local purposes. Moorstone lying loose on the surface of the Moor is abundant, strong and of a suitable size for use. Although it was used in its rough form over 5,500 years ago, it was not until well into the Middle Ages that men learnt how to dress the stone with any accuracy. However, a granite 'industry' was not established until the 19th century. In the 1820's the first major granite quarries were established on Dartmoor at Haytor (1820) and Foggintor / Swell Tor (1823).

Aerial view of the main quarry at Haytor.

(Simon Dell)

Both of these sites are accessible, close to moorland routes that enabled downhill transport, and were chosen as much for their proximity to readily available transport (Stover Canal and the Plymouth & Dartmoor Railway), as they were because of the quality of the granite they realized.

Some quarries were large commercial operations, such as those at Haytor and Walkhampton Common, but others were opened for specific requirements, like Heckwood Tor for the Plymouth Breakwater and Venford Quarry for the reservoir which supplies water to Paignton.

A pair of back-to-back bankers located near the tramway beside Foggintor Quarry.

(Simon Dell)

Although Haytor had declined by the time of greatest demand for setts, a small quantity of kerbstones were produced there by Easton & Son in the late 1880's. At the same time the large quarries at Foggintor and Swell Tor were in vigorous production under John & William Johnson. In response to the rapidly increasing demand, and contracts to supply setts, kerbstones and channelling to Plymouth and London, the Johnsons (latterly Pethick Brothers) and others also began to explore the feasibility of production at a number of other sites, including Dewerstone, Ingra Tor (where setts were made until as late as 1941), Criptor and Pew Tor (an especially important source of stone from a lower, more hospitable level). In 1862 Pew Tor was leased by John Greenwood, producing kerbstones, after which the lease lapsed until 1874 when William Duke, who had been working moorstone at Great Staple Tor opened up Merrivale Quarry, working both Great Staple Tor and Pew Tor setts together. Opposite Merrivale Quarry the small Grey Dawn Quarry was opened in the 1930's to produce setts and kerbstones. Great expense was frequently incurred removing overburden and weathered rock to reach sound granite. Attempts to open up Merrivale Quarry nearly failed because of this expense in 1883.

In many quarries – particularly the larger, more commercial operations - sett making was perceived as a way of dealing with the problem of disposing of waste rock unsuitable for the larger blocks required for construction or engineering works, rather than a purely commercial product in their own right. When setts became unfashionable some granite was crushed for road stone.

The commercial production of setts on Dartmoor was not entirely successful, consequently very short lived, and by the late 1880's almost all production of granite setts had ceased, however small quantities were produced for some time after to satisfy purely local needs. The demise of the industry was not because of loss of demand for setts, although markets were dwindling, but from outside competition. Records exist of setts being made in a large variety of locations throughout the UK. In 1833 leases were granted for the production of setts at Penmaenmawr in Wales, to be transported as ballast on ships bound for Liverpool.

Sett makers from Penmaenmawr granite quarry
in the early twentieth century.
(Courtesy of Emma @ Penmaenmawr.com)

In 1873 English sett makers from Rothley, Mountsorrel and Hartshill quarries near Leicester were employed by the Dalbeattie firm of Curteis and Shearer. Mention can be found of sett making at Huncote and Sapcote at around the same time. In all of these areas it was outcrops of igneous rocks, particularly granite but occasionally darker igneous rocks such as produced in the Winn Sill, which were worked to produce road stones.

In the latter years of the 19th century thousands of tons of granite setts and kerbstones were imported from the Channel Islands, especially Jersey, and from the Wicklow mountains in Ireland. In 1903 Pethick Brothers lost the contract to supply kerbstones and channelling for London to Norwegian competitors, where labour costs were less, overburden sparse, the granite easier to work and fjord-side quarries made direct shipment easy. Sett making in the South-West was never as important as it was in Aberdeen, Mountsorrel and the Channel Isles where the hard-wearing granites were considered among the best quality for street setts. Interestingly, at none of these locations is there any mention of structures similar to the bankers which occur over large areas of Dartmoor and Bodmin Moor. And so it was that this peculiarly south-west industry, with men stooping over small granite benches chipping away at blocks of stone faded as quickly as it arose. Driven into obscurity by competition and reduced demand. The final death knell came to many of the labour-intensive industries such as quarrying with the outbreak of the First World War, when large numbers of young men saw an opportunity to escape the hardship which was the lot of most men who worked the moors at this time.

A banker used to re-work stone from within a cairn on Twelve Men's Moor on Bodmin Moor

(Simon Dell)

Above: English Stonecrop (Sedum anglicum) flourishes on the arid granite spoil of most of the bankers.

(Simon Dell)

Below: A banker inside a collapsed stone built shelter near Yellowmead Farm at Fogintor, on the slopes of North Hessary Tor.

(Simon Dell)

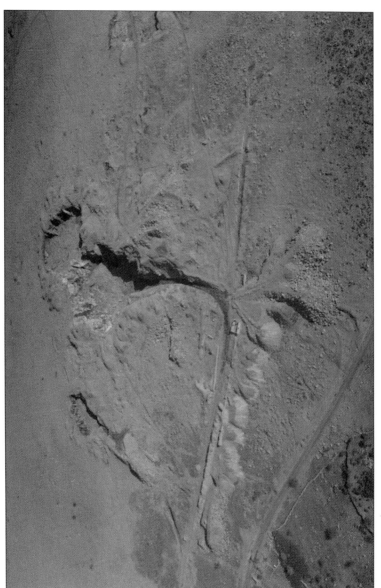

Aerial photograph of Swelltor Quarry workings, with the railway line of the Princetown Branch clearly in the lower left. The quarry siding runs across from left to right above the spoil heaps.
(Simon Dell with kind permission of Maristow Estates Office)

Foggintor Quarry clearly showing the ruins of the quarry building complex known as Hill Cottages. (Simon Dell with kind permission of Maristow Estates Office)

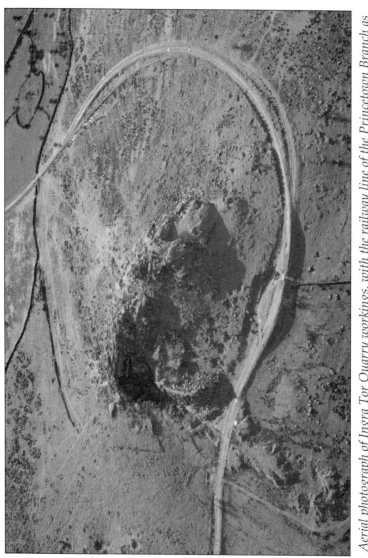

Aerial photograph of Ingra Tor Quarry workings, with the railway line of the Princetown Branch as it loops its way around the tor base. The area of the quarry spoils heaps are at the bottom left of the photograph where the 'standing' banker is located.

(Simon Dell with kind permission of Maristow Estates Office)

36

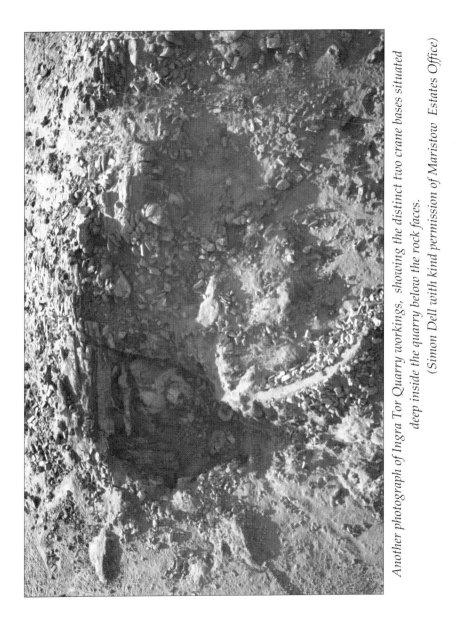

Another photograph of Ingra Tor Quarry workings, showing the distinct two crane bases situated deep inside the quarry below the rock faces.

(Simon Dell with kind permission of Maristow Estates Office)

*Middle Staple Tor with Merrivale Quarry in the foreground
showing the large crane, now dismantled and removed.
(Simon Dell with kind permission of the Duchy Estates Office)*

Holwell Quarry near Haytor. Showing the long incline of the Granite Tramway leading down the steep hill, as well as 'Rubble Heap Quarry' at the top of the photograph.

(Simon Dell)

Above: A moss-covered banker situated in Dewerstone Woods.
(Simon Dell)
Below: One of the many bankers located near the quarry at Lowery,
south of Peak Hill.
(Simon Dell)

Another view of Great Staple Tor with the causeway distinctively running across its eastern slopes. (Simon Dell with kind permission of the Duchy Estates Office)

4. HOW WERE THE SETTS MADE?

The sett making "industry" on Dartmoor was short-lived, restricted to only a small geographical area of the moor, and seen by quarry managers as a means of generating income from waste rock which otherwise would have needed disposal. Apart from the small bankers which litter areas of the south-west moor, the cobbled streets in many areas of Plymouth and West Devon, and the large piles of cobbles stored in Highways Department yards, little remains to record the work of large numbers of men who stooped for hours each day chipping away at small blocks of hard granite.

Granite Setts of a back-lane in the city of Plymouth; showing the running slabs for the cart wheels to travel on down the hill.

(Simon Dell)

Nevertheless, by examining more complete records from other parts of the country where the same industry was carried out we can understand that the process was labour intensive and highly skilled.

The sett makers on Dartmoor seem to have operated as one integral part of a small team. The other important member was the man who cut and supplied the roughly trimmed blocks which the sett maker split and further trimmed to produce the finished article. Large pieces of quarried granite or surface stone were broken and cut to a size roughly 45cm. x 22cm with a thickness of 12cm; these were taken by the sett makers and cut to smaller sizes. Ample evidence of this can be found on the moor; close to a banker will be found a flat area covered with large, uneven granite chippings with no evidence that any fine or finishing work was carried out in the same location. This account of road stone manufactured from the Great Whin Sill lends further support:

"Selected stone at the face is roughly trimmed into blocks and then sent by the "blockers" to the sett makers who split and trim them to the shape and sizes required."

Typically, the size of sett cut from these blocks would have been 20cm x 12cm x 10cm.

Prior to 1800, granite was cut using the wedge-and-groove method: a line of grooves was cut with the point of a pick to a depth of about 8 cm, 12 cm long and about 8cm apart. Wooden wedges were inserted, soaked with water and allowed to expand overnight to split the stone evenly.

Above: A pair of bankers located deep inside Foggintor Quarry amongst the spoil heaps.

(Simon Dell)

Below: A group of four bankers on the eastern slopes of Middle Staple Tor.

(Simon Dell)

Right: An abandoned piece of granite on the slopes of Belstone Tor, showing evidence of an attempt to split the stone using the 'wedge and groove' method.

(Simon Dell)

The subsequent method of splitting granite using feather and tares was speedier. A line of holes about 8 cm deep and up to 30 cm apart was made with a 'jumper'. Into each hole was placed a narrow tapered iron wedge or 'tare' between two half-round iron 'feathers'. When the plugs were struck evenly the stone would split. It would undoubtedly have been this method that was employed by the "blockers" when cutting stone to supply the sett makers. The speed at which a line of holes could be bored using jumpers was surprisingly fast. At Carnsew in Cornwall in the 1880's George Harris found that 113 blows produced a hole of 7 cm. At Cheesewring it was reported that a group of 4 men cut a block of 2 cubic metres in fifteen minutes.

A display of the 'Feather and Tare' method of splitting granite
— located at Catle Drogo, near Drewsteignton
(Simon Dell by kind permission of the National Trust)

Stone can be split in any of three ways to form blocks:

"Capping" – splitting off the top of the rock parallel to the horizontal pseudo-bedding plane.

"Cleaving" – along a 'cleaving line' said by stone cutters to lie in the direction identified by the general orientation of the large feldspar crystals.

(The process of foliation makes crystals orientate in one direction perpendicular to the direction of pressure within the granite. Although the feldspar crystals – being the largest – were easiest to see, all crystals in the granite would have oriented in the same plane.)

"Tough way" – across the cleaving line.

The large feldspar crystals (phenocrysts) in Dartmoor granite make splitting the stone particularly difficult; they act in the stone in a very similar way to knots in wood, changing the direction of cleavage in often unpredictable ways. Anybody who walks on the moor will have seen numbers of moorstones where someone has clearly spent time working at splitting the rock only to be forced to abandon the effort when the stone split along a different line to the one planned. Clearly the "blocker" was as skilled in the working of stone as was his partner at the banker.

In a previous chapter we discussed how the sett maker could have positioned himself when working at the banker, concluding that he stood with his knees resting against the top of the bench, stooping over to work on the stone. The simple ergonomics of using often heavy hand tools is easier when standing than kneeling.

Sett makers used a variety of hammers to reduce small blocks of stone to the required size. The mall would have been used to mark a line all around the block, using quite gentle strikes to create a line of weakness in the same way that a glass cutter scores a sheet of glass. One final firm strike along the line would split the block. A muckle for removing excess and a dressing hammer for smoothing sharp edges would have completed the task in a relatively short time. It has been recorded that one man could produce 2 tons of setts per week using these tools. However, payment was by the number of useable setts cut - one (old) penny per sett. It was an extremely good worker who could cut sixty a day in order to earn five shillings.

The Blacksmith's shop at Swelltor Quarry. Note the large boulder to the right of the building with the holes — used to hold chisels for sharpening
(Simon Dell)

Generally around forty setts a day would be an average. Time was clearly of the essence in order to maximize income. Consequently the sett makers needed to keep the edges of their steel tools sharp and properly tempered, skills which required a blacksmith. Around Walkhampton Common the earliest stone workers would have used the blacksmith's shop at Pew Tor, although John Grenwood's smithy at Barn Hill (built in the 1860's at a cost of £80) was constructed to service the sett and kerbstones making industry around the Staple Tors and Merrivale areas. Latterly they would have used the blacksmith's shop at Merrivale Quarry, situated inside the main quarry complex and not out on the open hillside.

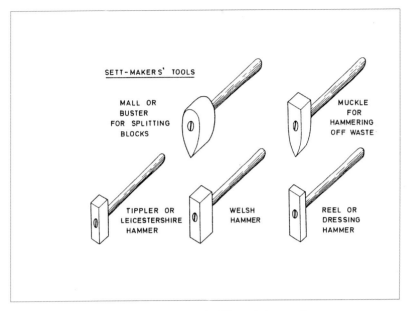

*Drawing of sett makers tools. The original tools are on
display in an outhouse at Castle Drogo.*
(Reproduced by courtesy of Peter Stannier)

There is a suggestion that sett making moved inside Merrivale
Quarry when it opened in the 1880's. However, there is no
evidence of bankers within the quarry. Maybe this is not
surprising. It was in full-scale use until very recently, and any
banker would have been destroyed as extraction continued.
We should also consider the possibility that the transition
to sett making within the quarry was accompanied by a
change in technique of manufacture. Certainly, the use of
small bankers to make setts appears to have been restricted
to the granite industry in the South West. In no other part of
the country where setts were made is any mention made to
a structure similar to a banker. It is possible that sett makers

employed a technique similar to that employed by their peers in Wales:

"The Welsh sett maker .... stands at his job, using his right foot as a third hand. He uses no tool but a heavy, pointed sledge, varying his stroke to suit his needs; some strokes so light would hardly crush a fly, followed by a crushing blow which splits a block of granite a couple of feet thick. Setts are trimmed by sledge work to given sizes, each size to a fixed gauge in length, breadth and thickness. The craftsman does all this measure by eye – no foot rule or other mechanical measurements for him. And he never varies a quarter of an inch in the measurement of his completed sett. I saw him at work. Supplied with a block of granite three or four times the size required, he was directed to show how it was done. Placing the block flat on the ground he marked by slight taps where the block should be split. One single blow followed – the block separated as evenly and cleanly as though cut by a knife. Adjusting one of the pieces with his foot he repeated the operation with three blows respectively for length, breadth and thickness and then pushed it with his foot to me. My companion, the working manager, handed me his two foot rule. I measured – and each measurement was well within the quarter inch [6mm] margin allowed. Here again efficiency spelt economy. Each man has his own shed, well constructed, strongly roofed, affording good shelter in all weathers."
('Industrial Wales Supplement' - 11th November 1921)

There are no bankers in or near the small Grey Dawn Quarry which was opened in the 1930's specifically to produce setts and kerbstones, but there is evidence that small sheds once stood on the site. It would seem safe to suggest that perhaps by then at least sett making had developed to mirror the techniques of other more successful quarries elsewhere.

A banker located in the upper 'Blue Elvan' quarry at Swelltor.
(Simon Dell)

Sett making was hard, demanding work. Although it was not as dangerous to life as the quarrying with which it was usually associated, accounts from elsewhere describe the injuries to hands, arms and face caused by shards of flying granite, and the scarring that these wounds left, particularly around the face. The Welsh sett making industry lasted longer than most, and a personal account from those times illustrates what effect sett making had on a worker:

"I can remember that Will the sett maker always wore the side out of his boot before the soles. He worked with others in small huts in the old Graigllyd quarry. I can also remember him telling me that on one occasion he visited Dr Ellis. The doctor said, "I see that you're a sett maker Mr. Williams". "Dew how did you know that?" "I can tell by the scarring on your eyes". (Personal account of Dae Hutton)

No safety glasses in those days of course! It was also in many places a transitory industry, with workers moving around the country as quarries opened and closed throughout the late 19th and early 20th centuries. At its height many thousands of men were employed in the industry, and certainly in areas such as Dalbeattie in Scotland these "causey-men" were amongst the highest paid of granite workers, much of which is attributed to the presence of a well-conducted trade union. Although the Sett Makers Union of Great Britain and Ireland was undoubtedly effective at representing its members, it could do little about the decline of the industry in the South West as demand dwindled and efficiency improved elsewhere, although it certainly tried. In 1901 as an example it objected to a reduction in the rates for sett manufacture at De Lank in Cornwall. The result of the objection is not

actually recorded, but like everywhere else in the South-West sett making at De Lank ceased soon after.

Left: The wheel-wright's stone at the ruins of Barn Hill Blacksmiths shop.
(Simon Dell)

5. TRANSPORTATION AND THE USE OF SETTS

The men who were toiling out in all weathers on the open moorland, cutting granite to supply their sett making colleagues with roughly shaped blocks, found themselves having to go wherever a plentiful supply of useful stone existed. Likewise, their sett making colleagues had to walk to wherever the raw material lay. Consequently their activities were spread over large areas, which were isolated and exposed. Some were able to utilize already-quarried stone such as at Foggintor and in the area of Swelltor, but on the slopes of Great Staple Tor and Leather Tor it was the rough moorstone which was used for making the setts.

In *'A handbook for Travellers in Devon and Cornwall'* by John Murray, published in London in 1851 Murray writes:

"...they swarm with men busily employed in breaking up the ponderous material with their iron instruments, while others are scattered far and wide over the huge side of North Hessary Tor, protected by reed covered frames, and preparing the surface blocks for removal".

Right: Banker within a granite built 'shaker' at Foggintor.

(Simon Dell)

As a result, the issue of transporting the completed setts from fairly remote areas was not one to be taken lightly, and much effort went into organizing their removal from the place of manufacture. It was clear from the beginning that tracks, tramways, incline planes and loading bays would need to be constructed to support the industry.

The sett making production was at its height in the 1870, prior to the steam engine railway being brought up to Princetown. Instead, this was the period of Thomas Tyrwhitt's horse-drawn tramway, which served the village from the port of Plymouth. Iron rails (this was Devon's first iron railroad) were laid upon granite sleepers in a tortuous and winding route across the open moors.

Unfortunately no known photographs have come to light of the wagons pulled by the horses or any contemporary images of the former tramway line being used, although photography did exist, albeit in its infancy, during that period. One of the only known images of the tramway is that of a beautiful freeze around a roof light and wall at Tor Royal Farm near Princetown. This shows the carriages of the tramway, constructed by Thomas Tyrwhitt in the early years of the 19th Century, and it was at Tor Royal that Tyrwhitt made his home.

Left: The freeze showing Tyrwitt's Tramway located at Tor Royal Farm, Princetown. (Courtesy of Paul Rendell)

For those sett makers re-using the cut stone at Foggintor the problem of transportation was easily overcome with the close proximity of the tramway wagons. The tramway also served the sett makers at Swell Tor and King's Tor, who wouldn't have had far to take their setts to the wagons. For the sett makers working on the slopes of North Hessary, above Yellowmead Farm, an extension of the horse drawn tramway was built northwards in order to access the open moors between Foggintor and the Tavistock to Princetown road near the present-day area known as Fourwinds. Some bankers still exist on these slopes, some with rough granite built shakers. Obviously the reed-covered frames seen by Murray in the 1850s have long since gone, but the men no doubt supplemented their granite structures with corrugated iron when available.

The Foggintor Track with the old tramway granite sleepers.
(Simon Dell)

There is also a standing banker at Ingra Tor quarry spoil tip, but this would have probably dates from the period of the steam railway. Its construction is similar in many respects to the bankers within Portland Quarry in Dorset, where men stood upright to work at their benches.

It is, however, upon the slopes of Great Staple Tor that the ingenuity of the granite workers is really clear to see. With their area of work being so remote from proper transport they had a fair distance to transport their setts. It was here that the moorstone was levered aside to clear a route to make rough tracks and causeways.

The granite workers' causeway leading northwards across the slopes of Middle Staple Tor to Great Staple Tor.

(Simon Dell)

These tracks were subsequently used to bring a horse-drawn wagon as close to the area of manufacture as possible. Throughout the slopes on the southern and eastern sides of Great Staple and Middle Staple Tors the hillside is criss-crossed with the evidence of these cart tracks. The carts themselves were single axle wagons, pulled by one stout horse, invariably a Shire. The wheels were a set distance apart and the axle was also a set height above the ground.

Horse and cart similar to those used to remove setts from the places of manufacture on the open moors.

(Simon Dell collection)

Once the cart arrived as near as possible to the pile of newly cut setts it would be hauled and reversed into two parallel groves cut into the hillside. These grooves formed a rudimentary platform upon which the cart was parked so that it was flat and secure. At the rear end of the grooves the cart was reversed up against a granite block or high bank which formed a loading platform so that the setts could be easily placed onto the flat bed of the cart. Sometimes if the ground was particularly sloping the grooves were quite deeply cut into the ground, barely room enough for the axel to fit above the earth. Once the cart was loaded, the horse could pull it out from the loading bay and onto the nearby track and thus onwards to the main roadway for eventual transportation into Tavistock. The sides of the tors here at Great Staple and Middle Staple Tors are littered with evidence of these individual loading bays.

The loading bay grooves, for the wheels of the carts to rest in,
with Middle Staple Tor in the distance.

(Simon Dell)

Along the eastern side of the slope leading from Middle Staple to Great Staple there is a well constructed and significant track way or causeway used by horse-pulled carts to access the bankers on that flank of the hill. This was associated as well as, no doubt, with the previous large scale removal of moorstone prior to the opening of Merrivale Quarry in the mid 1870's (then known simply as Tor Quarry).

The causeway leading up to the area of bankers on the southern slopes of Leather Tor, above Burrator Reservoir.

(Simon Dell)

In the other areas of sett manufacture similar tracks and causeways have been built. On the southern slopes of Leather Tor, above Burrator Reservoir, there are a number

59

of tracks as well as a significant causeway. Loading bays also exist to support the use of horse-drawn carts accessing the slopes where the rough moorstone was used in the sett making industry. In the neighbouring Lowery Stent Quarry area on the southern slopes of Peek Hill there is evidence of use of both moorstone and also quarry spoil in making setts. Some of the large bankers in this area have rough tracks leading to them with boulders rolled aside to gain access. Loading bays also litter the hillside nearby.

The incline tramway in the woods at Dewerstone, near Shaugh Prior, servicing the quarries and bankers that litter the hillside.

(Simon Dell)

No such loading bays exist in the woods above Shaugh Bridge near the Dewerstone. In this area a sophisticated tramway and noteworthy incline plane was built to access the small quarries built into the hillside high above the river. The area is now in woodland and much of the evidence of the flourishing granite industry, which took place here has been lost under vegetation.

A moss-covered large banker in Dewerstone Woods high up in the area of the three quarries.

(Simon Dell)

The sett makers' bankers in this area are confined to the high area above the incline plane and below the side of the upper horizontal tramway line leading from the cable drum building to the quarries. Most of the bankers are now covered in thick moss amongst the trees, but they all lie within easy reach of the tramway. Both moorstone and quarry spoil could have easily been accessible for the sett makers' use. The tramway in the area never was coupled to the main Plymouth to Tavistock line of the later railway although grand plans had existed for that connection to be made.

Similar use of loading bays and cart tracks also existed on the neighbouring area of Bodmin Moor. Clearly systems of work and methods of transportation were common throughout the area of Dartmoor and Bodmin Moor where setts were being made, whether using moorstone or quarry spoil.

Once removed from whichever area, the setts were used predominantly in the Plymouth Borough or Tavistock areas. A walk around Tavistock will soon lead you to back lanes, which are either in their original state of being paved with setts, or alternatively where refurbishment has taken place, where setts have been re-used as modern day road and path surface. Likewise there are many areas in Plymouth city where setts are still in existence. Areas especially close to HM Dockyard, where in some areas, thousands of setts are stockpiled for use within historic conservation areas in the dockyard. Other areas of the city still paved with setts are near Bretonside Bus Station and also near Freedom Fields Park in the access lanes behind Victorian terraces, as well as in the back lanes at the rear of the Pennycomequick public house.

In the following chapter we will detail where you might be able to visit areas where sett makers bankers still exist.

6. THE PRESENT

"Well, where can I go and find all these ruins of sett making of long ago?" you are no doubt asking. In this last chapter we will be describing what evidence you are likely to be able to find for yourselves connected with the work of the Sett Makers. Firstly there is an excellent display in a shed at Castle Drogo, showing hand tools used by the workers who dressed and cut the granite. The castle is well worth a visit in its own right, but the display is one of the best in the locality of Dartmoor. The National Trust manages the property and an entrance fee applies.

The display shed at Castle Drogo, showing the tools used by the granite workers and sett makers.
(Simon Dell courtesy of the National Trust)

Left: The display of granite workers' tools at castle Drogo.
(Simon Dell courtesy of The National Trust)

Throughout these pages we have mentioned that setts adorn many streets throughout Tavistock, Plymouth and beyond. Particularly nice examples are to be found in the back lanes around Freedom Fields Park in Plymouth as well as to the rear of the public house at Pennycomequick in the city. In Tavistock setts are used in a few newly restored areas such as Church Lane beside the Parish Church in the town centre as well as existing sites including the footpath which leads off Barley Market Street to the rear of the Town Council Offices.

Bankers on Dartmoor and Bodmin Moor are found in a variety of locations. On Bodmin there are a couple of nice ones situated in the Cheesewring Quarry above Minions. If you enter the main quarry along the old tramway line you turn left and go along a grassy path with spoil heaps on your left. There are two bankers built into the spoil heaps at the side of the pathway. There are also some built into cairns on Twelvemen's Moor above the quarry.

On Dartmoor there are numerous locations. On the edge of the National Park in Grenofen woods there are some near the quarry. To reach this location, go down the lane opposite the Halfway Public House at Grenofen and turn second left (ignoring the private first left leading to Grenofen Manor itself). At the bottom of the narrow lane you cross the river and park on the right (SX 489 709). Walk back over the river and turn left along a footpath leading to Doublewaters. Once you have passed by the house on your left and gone through the pedestrian gate into the woods you reach a well made very high wall on your right retaining spoil from the quarries above you in the trees. The bankers are at the top and edge of this high wall over looking the river (SX 487 707).

A 'standing banker' located at Ingra Tor, in the spoil heaps north of the Ingra Tor Railway Halt ruins..

(Simon Dell)

Again, on the edge of the National Park in Dewerstone woods there are several high up in the woods. Park at Shaugh Bridge (SX 533 636) and walk over the wooden footbridge and along the well cobbled path, leading uphill into the woods. The path turns left and follows the line of an old tramway parallel with the River Meavy. Continue along the track until the incline plane (SX 536 641). Go up the incline plane to the ruined winch building (SX 537 642) and turn sharp right along the higher tramway line. This leads to several quarries on your left located along the line. The bankers are all situated below this upper tramway in the clitter and moss in the trees. There are a few also located opposite the quarry mouths, below the tramway line.

Left: One of the three Dewerstone Quarries. (Simon Dell)

By far the largest group of bankers can be found on the south and eastern slopes of the Staple Tor complex. It is best to park in the car park located on the left between Cox Tor car park and Merrivale (SX 539 749). Leaving the car look north towards Middle Staple Tor. There is a tree about 100 metres ahead. Walk towards the tree and from here simply hunt about in the boulders all about the tree and towards Merrivale Quarry and you will come across several dozen bankers. On the slopes there are also the ruins of buildings and the rude shelters of stone used by the sett makers. There are also a number of loading bays for horse drawn carts in the area. The second area is to the east of Middle Staple Tor. Walk around to the old explosives store ruin above the quarry at Merrivale and head north with Middle Staple Tor on your left. An easy path can be found along the line of a dry leat, the forerunner of the present day Grimstone & Sortridge Leat. There are the best examples uphill to your left, including 'fours' and 'fives' all in a line. Above you towards Great Staple Tor you can see the line of the causeway leading up to the highest banker tucked under Great Staple Tor itself. There are a few broken examples near the top of Middle Staple Tors on its eastern side. Below the dry leat is also an area of boulders and clitter. There are numerous bankers dotted about in this difficult to access and ankle-twisting area.

A rather odd banker can be found (SX 548 758) below the present day leat near to the track leading to Shillapark Farm. It consists of a large banker and moulded seat, where the sett maker can tuck his legs underneath and work in comfort at a bench. It does not follow the designs of the older bankers so might well be a much later example.

Other locations of a large amount of bankers can be found at Foggintor – both inside the quarry and around the railway line at its edge as well as in the spoil heaps. Park at the end of the Yellowmead Farm track (SX 567 749) and walk past the farm towards the quarry. Once you have passed the farm keep a sharp lookout on your left for evidence of a sett built into a rubble heap. Other examples are around the edge of the railway tramline on the left once you have passed the ruins at the quarry entrance. These are built into the bottom of the spoil heaps and can be located by looking for the telltale signs of rubble and granite chippings. There is even one built at the top of the spoil heap above the ruined blacksmith's building at the southern boggy entrance of the quarry.

If you go into the quarry itself from the entrance opposite the large ruins on Big Tip, go right in and pass the pond.

The 'seated banker' near Shillapark Farm at Merrivale. With moulded granite seat where the sett maker could comfortably sit to use the bench.
(Simon Dell)

Continue into the far end of the quarry below the highest faces of all on the left and you will find a few bankers used by men re-working spoil inside the quarry. There are also several nice crane-bases in the area.

The very ruinous banker on the south side of King's Tor, in the lower middle part of the photograph, with its top missing.

(Simon Dell)

Upon leaving the quarry continue along the tramway line towards King's Tor Halt (SX565 732). On your right are many spoils heaps and there are bankers built into the bases as well as on the very tops of these heaps. There are also bankers on the open flat ground past the heaps as you approach the main GWR Railway line ahead of you at King's Tor Halt.

A short walk to King's Tor itself will locate another very ruinous banker on the south side of the summit, protected by a large face of rock about 2 metres high. We didn't locate any more than this one banker on King's Tor – but that might give you a good reason to search about the area to locate more!

Once you have visited King's Tor stroll along the railway line to Swelltor Quarry. Go along the line and past the large building ruin on the right (SX558 731). Carry on about 50 metres and start climbing up to the left. There are spoil and rubble heaps all about here with a number of bankers tucked into them. There are also bankers in both the quarries as well as above the quarries on the edges of the tramway lines.

If you are feeling energetic, once having visited Swelltor you could always stroll around to Ingra Tor quarry (SX 555 721) with its two lovely crane bases.

Left: The two distinctive circular crane bases located at the back of Ingra Tor quarry. The line of the Princetown Railway (formerly the horse drawn tramway) cuts across the entrance of the quarry. In the distance are the quarry spoil heaps where the single 'standing banker' is located.

(Simon Dell)

However, if you come out of the quarry and cross the railway line, through the gate to the spoil heaps there is a high standing banker in the heap. Obvious evidence of use exists but whether it is old enough to have been a sett making banker is debatable.

The final area to mention is the Peek Hill and Leather Tor area. There are two sites of bankers on this hillside. Firstly at Lowery Stent quarry (SX 555 696) where there are some in the slopes leading into the gully below the quarry and also beside the numerous track ways to the south west of the main quarry itself, in the trees. There are some really big examples above the trees south west of Peek Hill.

Right: One of the very large 'Lowery Stent' bankers on the southerly slopes of Peek Hill over looking Burrator Reservoir. (Simon Dell)

Over to the east on Leather Tor a good access point is at Cross Gate and along the laneway beside the Devonport Leat. Once the lane goes over the leat turn left and go uphill along the clitter strewn slopes of the lower part of Leather Tor. Several bankers are to be found right across this hillside. The men had clearly used the moorstone here because there is no evidence of quarrying in the areas of the bankers.

We have searched on the eastern side of Dartmoor in the Haytor Quarry complex but could not find any bankers. This might be because of the fact that the main period of the sett making industry came about long after the closure of the Haytor Quarry complex. We would however welcome any further sightings of bankers from readers and we can be reached via the publisher.

Hopefully these chapters, whilst not comprehensive or purporting to be a definitive list of all bankers, might have inspired the reader to go out and search for himself for these wonderful memorials to men of a bygone industrial age. They are truly epitaphs to the rugged and stoic lives of granite workers whose lives of hardship and toil surely eclipse the conditions that 21st century workers have to contend with.

Left: A recently restored two wheeled cart of the type used by the sett makers. With the high axel which allowed the wheels to roll into the platform grooves on the hillside.

(Gerald Williams)

7. LOCATIONS OF BANKERS

Below is laid out a list of the main sites of the bankers and locations in ten-figure grid references for ease of locating with a GPS. All grid references should be prefixed on a GPS with the letters SX.

Foggintor

56568	73508	Intact standing banker with 'stooper' attached
56570	73476	Banker at the entrance to the quarry
56610	73562	Intact banker opposite engine house
56624	73590	Intact banker NE of engine house
56681	73427	Banker inside quarry
56684	73472	Broken banker showing sorting
56687	73459	Banker inside quarry
56707	73549	Banker set into spoil heap
56713	74132	Setts / kerbstones manufactured
56737	74084	Single banker with evidence of stone shaker

Dewerstone

53704	64066	Banker inside enclosure with another possible in the same enclosure
53712	64101	Intact banker inside stone shaker

Ingra Tor

32767	72283	Standing banker on east side of spoil heap

King's Tor

32767	73858	Ruined banker on south side of main Tor

Leather Tor

56305	69634	Banker W of quarry
56331	69606	Banker on E side of quarry spoil heap
56334	69620	Intact banker inside small quarry
56446	69771	Intact banker facing ENE
56463	69779	Banker with top removed

Lowery Tor

55460	69595	Within clitter field
55477	69581	Within clitter field
55480	69578	In clitter
55490	69570	Knee recess less well pronounced
55492	69578	Flat top
55512	69574	Between lower and upper quarry
55513	69585	Flat top
55518	69566	Further back from quarry. Overgrown
55520	69525	Back of quarry in clitter field
55528	69532	W side of quarry
32767	69528	Edge of quarry facing East

Great Staple and Middle Staple Tors

53894	75253	Wide banker with one upright
53894	75272	Intact single
53933	75286	Double
53973	75288	2 singles together
54009	75246	Single in enclosure

54027	75247	Intact single
54035	75250	Large single
54036	75301	Single in enclosure
54041	75387	Back to back pair
54042	75288	Two singles in pit
54043	75299	Large double
54055	75347	Two singles
54060	75292	Large double
54068	75362	Intact single inside shaker
54068	75364	Intact single inside shaker
54083	75368	Ruined single in shaker
54084	75312	Back to back four
54088	75318	Collapsed single
54088	75338	Row of four
54090	75269	Quadruple with single nearby
54090	75309	Double
54091	75363	Single in enclosure
54092	75387	Ruined single in shaker
54097	75348	Single in enclosure
54098	75204	Large single
54102	75214	Single
32767	75352	Shaker containing two, with single nearby
54104	75248	Intact single
54105	75223	Single
54108	75196	Single
54113	75271	Collapsed single
54135	75339	Large single
54149	75348	Large single

54161	75314	Long single
54191	75365	Large single
54223	75391	Collapsed single
54232	75332	Double
54424	75710	Intact single
54462	75507	Collapsed row of four
54486	75509	Stripped single
54492	75512	Single with collapsed top
54497	75518	Intact single
54498	75516	Intact single
54498	75528	Good condition double
54499	75682	Disturbed single
54501	75520	Intact single
54512	75615	Single
54519	75670	Two singles together
54525	75457	Collapsed single
54529	75450	Double at 90 degrees to each other
54530	75623	Collapsed single
54532	75487	Triple
54533	75477	Two singles together
54563	75464	Large single
54565	75781	Unusual double
54572	75594	Two singles together
54578	75458	Collapsed single
54578	75460	Back to back pair
54590	75610	Disturbed single
54593	75571	Large single
54597	75487	Collapsed single
54606	75511	Large single
54606	75514	Intact single

54614	75570	Single
54614	75796	Collapsed single
54618	75504	Intact single
54622	75487	Collapsed single
54633	75485	Two singles together
54642	75493	Two singles together
54684	75604	Intact single
54695	75523	Two singles, partially collapsed
54709	75623	Single in enclosure
54715	75622	Single
54716	75577	Intact single
54722	75608	Intact single
54731	75560	Single
32767	75681	Single

Swell Tor

56009	73123	Single in shaker
56030	73346	Single

Grenofen Quarry

32767	70811	Raised above pathway at wall's edge by the Elvan Quarry.

North Hessary Tor

32767	74128	East of the track passing Yellowmead Farm in a pile of waste.

This list is not intended to be an exhaustive and definitive schedule of all Dartmoor's Sett Makers' Bankers. It merely gives an indication where the large groups are located.

POST SCRIPT

Nineteenth century sett layers working on a cobbled roadway using the setts from local quarries..

(Courtesy of the National Trust of Guernsey and the Guernsey Folk Museum)

The manufacture of the setts by the sett makers out on the open moors is not the end of this story. The conclusion must rest with the men who laid the setts into magnificent hard-wearing road surfaces. Their job was as equally back-breaking as the men who made the setts. If this small book has left you wondering with admiration at the hardships and privations endured by the Dartmoor sett makers then their story was worth telling.

INDEX

Dartmoor's Sett Makers' Bankers has been serialised in the *Dartmoor News*, a bi-monthly magazine, available from selected retail outlets and some information centres. It can also be obtained direct by contacting Paul Rendell on 01837 54727 email: paul.dartmoor@virgin.net

Website: www.dartmoornews.co.uk

The co-author, Simon Dell, is a regular contributor to the magazine both with articles as well as a regular guided walk series.

THE AUTHORS

Simon Dell is a retired policeman and a Dartmoor National Park Guide who has spent over 40 years walking on Dartmoor. He was a member of the Dartmoor Rescue Group for almost half that time. He was awarded the MBE in 1997 for services to Dartmoor Rescue and the community. He has written a number of books on the subject of policing history and Dartmoor Prison and has appeared on television and radio, speaking on those subjects. He is a regular contributor to Dartmoor publications and magazines.

John Bright was born and raised in south-east London, and served as a policeman there throughout the riots and strikes of the eighties. Relocating to Wiltshire he worked for a few years as a gamekeeper before moving to the South West. In 1993 he graduated from Exeter University, since when he has been teaching Geology and Physics at two secondary schools in Plymouth. He has also taught Geology to undergraduates of the Open University.